DECLARATIONS

DECLARATIONS

a play by Jordan Tannahill

Coach House Books | Toronto

copyright © Jordan Tannahill, 2018

first edition

Published with the generous assistance of the Canada Council for the
Arts and the Ontario Arts Council. Coach House Books also acknowl-
edges the support of the Government of Canada through the Canada
Book Fund and the Government of Ontario through the Ontario Book
Publishing Tax Credit.

LIBRARY AND ARCHIVES CANADA CATALOGUING IN PUBLICATION

Tannahill, Jordan, author
        Declarations / Jordan Tannahill.

A play.
Issued in print and electronic formats.
ISBN 978-1-55245-359-9 (softcover).

        I. Title.

PS8639.A577D43 2018   C812'.6   C2017-905082-6

Declarations is available as an ebook: ISBN 978 1 77056 544 9 (EPUB),
978 1 77056 545 6 (PDF).

For my mother

Playwright's Note

Three years ago my mother was told she had less than three years to live. The news shattered me. My grief was all-consuming and yet I knew it wasn't special. We all live with the inevitability of losing everyone and everything. But how do we do this? It suddenly struck me as the most impossible task. And that we should continue living in the face of this impossibility seemed to me both an exquisite and somewhat absurd act of defiance.

Shortly after receiving my mother's news, I was on a six-hour plane ride home to visit her. While 35,000 feet in the air, I looked down at my hand and thought: this is my left hand. I whispered it to myself. *This is my left hand.* It felt edifying. As if, with those words, I was declaring: *for now, this too still exists.* I wrote *Declarations* in a single, fevered sitting on that plane ride, as if by picking through the fragments of myself – images, sounds, sensations – I would come to understand what constituted a life. Perhaps so as to better understand what it meant to lose one.

Declarations is driven by the desire to articulate the entirety of a life and the inherent impossibility of doing so. In a sense, all art occupies the space between human experience and our sublime failure to fully articulate human experience. I wanted to create a piece that spoke to that. To create an archive, fated to be woefully incomplete, of a life lived. In this case the life is mine, but through their embodiment of the text it also becomes that of the five performers.

Accompanying the text is a gestural score: the performers spontaneously generate gestures that embody and further illuminate each declaration. While the text is fixed, the performers' improvised movement keeps this archive a living one, changing night after night. In this way, the text passes through the prism of each performer's lived experience and refracts back a wholly unique and personal vision of a life.

A younger, more cynical version of myself would have been reluctant to say this, but fuck it: for me, live performance is a spiritual act. I do think of the theatre as a kind of temple. We go to the temple to grapple with the fundamental questions of the human condition. And for me, *Declarations* is a ritual for the temple. A means of processing the terror of death through the joyful evocation of life.

Jordan Tannahill
December 2017

Performance History

Declarations premiered at Canadian Stage's Berkeley Street Theatre on January 23, 2018. The production was directed by Jordan Tannahill, with the following creative team:

1: Liz Peterson
2: Jennifer Dahl
3: Danielle Baskerville
4: Philip Nozuka
5: Rob Abubo

Lighting Designer: Kimberly Purtell
Technical Director: Greg Dougherty
Stage Manager: A. J. Laflamme
Assistant Stage Manager: Ashley Ireland

Original vocal composition by Philip Nozuka, with the ensemble

Producer: Lynanne Sparrow
Technical Director: Greg Dougherty
Production Manager: Heather Landon
Director of Production: Lee Milliken
Senior Head Technician: Sally Roberts
Head of Wardrobe: Ming Wong

Artistic Director: Matthew Jocelyn
Interim Managing Director and Executive Producer: Sherrie Johnson

The Gestural Score

While the gestural score in *Declarations* is spontaneously generated each night, we arrived at fifteen rules for what the gestures could and could not be. I would encourage directors to use these rules as a starting point for their own interpretation of the piece, but also to feel at liberty to dispense with some and discover others.

• Gestures should be a genuine attempt to communicate the essence of each declaration.

• Simple is best.

• No acting.

• Avoid dance-like movements.

• Avoid facial expressions.

• Reset to a neutral physicality when possible, facing outward toward audience.

• Sometimes you will speak the declaration first, and then perform the gesture. Other times, you will speak the declaration and perform the gesture at the same time. It will largely depend on how quickly the gesture occurs to you.

• For every five or so simple gestures (i.e., one motion of the arm or hand), you may have a slightly longer, multi-part gesture (perhaps one that moves you through the space).

• 'Runs' are encouraged. 'Runs' are sequences in which you flow seamlessly between one declaration/gesture and another, as if each one were building off the last.

• Very occasionally you can make a sound to accompany a declaration/gesture, but only if that sound spontaneously arises from the execution of the gesture.

• No imitations of butterflies or birds.

• No finger symbols (i.e., a gun, a peace sign, the middle finger, etc.)

• Avoid pointing at the thing you are referring to; embody it.

• A variety of movement and stillness is crucial.

• So is levity and play.

Declarations

A bare stage, stripped of masking.

1 enters.

She stands for a moment.

She then proceeds to make a series of declarations, each accompanied by a gesture. The gesture is meant to illustrate the image or idea contained within the declaration. The gestures are governed by the fifteen rules set out on pages 7–8.

The text is fixed, but the gestures are not: the performers must rediscover each gesture afresh, night after night. The difficulty – and humour – inherent in this nightly feat of improvisation should emerge but not distract.

1: This is the thing

   This is not the thing

   This is my mother

   This is her eyelash

   This is a flag

   This is an empty promise

   This is the speed of light

   This is a chewed fingernail

   This is a pocket with a hole in it

   This is Saturn

This is political

This is the morning light

This is the morning light coming through the window

This is her body in the shower

This is the warm water falling

This is her dying breath

This is my heart in the morning

This is her laughter

This is her absence

This is the state of things to come

This is a dog

This is how I lie down

This is Ikea

This is a year

This is a child

This is a life

This is a street corner

This is a car speeding

This is the hard part

This is Tuesday

This is the colour red

This is the smell of freshly cut grass

This is the end of the world

This is me ignoring you at a party

This is time itself

This is my hand

This is me clapping

This is the distance between us

This is my father leaving when I was two

This is a swing set in the backyard

This is God

This is a plastic cup of apple juice

This is a shady street in the suburbs

This is a two-storey house with wall-to-wall carpet

This is life on Earth

This is the colour green

This is a witness

This is me wetting the bed until I was twelve

This is an erection

This is a secret

This is a weapon

This is me, coming apart at the seams

This is my first sexual encounter

This is a country

This is a map of the country

This is a scar

This is my mother on the beach

This is the length of a human tongue

This is a high school parking lot

This is the smokers' corner

This is physics

This is a forest full of beer bottles

This is the place where I lose you

This is snow

This is our neighbourhood

This is a motel

This is your uncle in his white briefs

This is my mother alone with her thoughts

This is the weight of the world

This is the funeral

This is a rim job

This is the earth seen from space

This is a lifelong fear of heights

This is a shitstorm

This is an animal made of papier-mâché

This is how we collapse

This is the future

This is a dirty rag

This is a ghost town

This is a deck of cards

This is the ace of spades

This is me spending time in the world

This is thirty seconds of your time

This is the shape you were looking for

This is my mother looking at Van Gogh

This is an overpriced salad

This is just my opinion

This is a cartoon version of myself

This is a remote island

This is a personal vendetta

This is me missing you

This is dawn

This is a shortcut

This is a sparrow

This is a midair collision

This is the colour blue

This is a film starring Juliet Binoche

This is a regret

This is an abandoned storefront

This is an opening

This is a complimentary snack

This is a tiny ball of cellophane

This is a prop in a play

This is my life compressed into ten seconds

This is an unremarkable blow job

This is a swimming pool in the desert

This is a trick the light plays

This is a precocious teenager

This is a walnut

This is a late-night karaoke regret

This is an important detail

This is a forest fire

This is a condo gym

This is fascism

This is an art opening

This is my mother's fear of elevators

This is laminate flooring

This is a stain on the wallpaper

This is a cupboard without a door

This is a basement apartment

This is how we made ends meet

This is the corner store

This is a can of evaporated milk

This is the ice storm

This is Satan

This is the letter 'A' in Times New Roman

This is a run in the stocking

This is Grade 4

This is recess

This is a recession

This is what's left

This is a raccoon named Debbie

This is the tide going out

This is the edge of the wilderness

This is my mother crying

This is her ghost

This is a baby who looks like an old man

This is my wedding

This is an optical illusion

This is the Pacific Ocean

This is a conference on queer theory

This is a nipple

This is the fifteenth century

This is cloud coverage

This is a macaron

This is a virulent strain of smallpox

This is the smell of my mother lingering in a closet

This is the year that came after

This is a song by Joni Mitchell

This is slapstick

This is a fresh coat of paint

This is a paper cut

This is the mirror after a hot shower

This is a brunch date

This is a confession

This is some unwarranted recognition

This is a bungalow

This is the colour yellow

This is a bully

This is an ice rink

This is Abraham and Isaac

This is the last sentence in a long book

This is an old sofa on the sidewalk

This is the reason

This is a dinner with friends

This is the second miscarriage

This is Grade 9

This is bad taxidermy

This is the boy who went missing

This is a spent bullet casing

This is a last-minute request

This is food poisoning

This is a passport application

This is a line in the sand

This is a piece of gum stuck to your shoe

This is a small baggie of drugs smuggled in a rectum

This is an old laptop in the closet

This is the equator

This is a sperm whale

This is a clue

This is the Cuban Missile Crisis

This is my birthmark

This is a sacrifice

This is Billie Holiday

This is the number eight

This is a fraction of the love I have to give

This is a demolition derby

This is a carton of milk

This is a slice of pizza

This is a joyride

This is a weak WiFi signal

This is a blunt object

This is an overly air-conditioned room

This is feminism

This is just a suggestion

This is where the horses go

This is a shipping crate of elephant tusks

This is a moment of respite

This is a place

This is a fact

This is me trying

This is my leaving

This is a louse

This is a seed

This is a fish

This is a table

This is a farmer

This is a leaf

This is a root

This is blood

This is bone

This is a crease

This is an egg

This is an eye

This is a horn

This is skin

This is a claw

This is a knee

This is a foot

This is hair

This is a breast

This is a neck

This is a belly

This is a hand

This is a liver

This is my good ear

This is water

This is a wave

This is stone

This is sand

This is smoke

This is a path

This is night

This is a mountain

This is a hill

This is cold

This is round

This is clean

This is goodbye

This is today

This is an estuary

This is an ossuary

This is a floodplain

This is a cove

This is a cave

This is a mesa

This is a mess

This is the sky

This is a good man

This is prom night

This is a backseat

This is a highway in Northern Ontario

This is the smell of beer on your breath

This is a bow-tie undone

This is a moose on the road

This is an antler

This is a leg

This is a windshield

This is blood from your nose

This is the shoulder of a highway

This is the end

This is nostalgia

This is an assassin

This is the assassination of JFK

This is a blurry photograph

This is the moon landing

This is my middle finger

This is punk rock

This is my mother's record collection

This is her dancing in the living room with the blinds drawn

This is the Big Bang

This is evolution

This is everything that came after

This is a coup d'état

This is blood on your hands

This is making love in the afternoon

This is my mother chopping onions

This is a dust mote

This is an eye infection

This is an eyebrow

This is a hidden tattoo

This is your runny nose after coming in from the winter cold

This is moisture

This is the void

This is an experiment in kinetics

This is a hot tub in Vegas

This is your clavicle

This is a missed opportunity

This is the time I've wasted

This is attrition

This is the national debt

This is a cliff battered by the ocean

This is an industrial park

This is a needle

This is thread

This is my family

This is a broken condom

This is June

This is the valley

This is a vagina

This is a whisk

This is a scent-free space

This is the boreal forest

This is a subatomic particle

This is a calculated risk

This is a hipster dad pushing his son on the swing

This is the colour purple

This is Sunday school

This is a root canal

This is a willow tree

This is an squid shooting ink

This is Huckleberry Finn

This is an avocado

This is my childhood

This is how I whisper in your ear

As 1 speaks, 2 enters. 2 joins in without interrupting the flow of movement and text.

1: This is my hand outstretched

2: This is the thing

1: This is us playing Sega Genesis

2: This is not the thing

1: This is the fall of America

2: This is you quitting your job

1: This is an exorcism

2: This is you working as a waitress

1: This is Wikipedia

2: This is how you met my father

1: This is the drive home

2: This is how it ended

1: This is a nightmare

2: This is the dust under my bed

1: This is a shit stain on my underwear

2: This is me crying uncontrollably in the train station

1: This is the first time we fucked without condoms

2: This is my life without me

2 stops gesturing. 1 continues to silently gesture for each of 2's declarations.

2: This is me avoiding your question

    This is me being unreasonable

    This is calamity

This is Hollywood

This is a gas station in the Mojave desert

1 and 2 gesture on their own lines.

1: This is my sweat

2: This is us fucking in the back seat

1: This is us caught in the rain

2: This is us being quiet together

1: This is the humidity

2: This is your breath

1: This is my breath

1 and 2 gesture on all lines.

1: This is an airplane shot down from the sky

This is the fart you wouldn't own up to

This is a murmuration of starlings

This is a false idol

2: This is a false idol

This is your gratitude

1: This is a non-fat latte

This is a finished basement

This is the stingray that killed Steve Irwin

2: This is the nightlife

1: This is a blood feud

2: This is an ergonomic office chair

1: This is a novel interrupted by the death of its author

1 and 2 gesture on all lines.

2: This is spring

This is my soul

This is the sound of distant construction

This is a boy singing to himself under his breath

This is daylight

This is my friend Shane in a coma

2 stops gesturing. 1 continues to gesture in silence.

2: This is the second time you've interrupted me

This is a discontinued cereal

This is an undiscovered colour

This is an indescribable shape

This is how I got over you

This is the first man who loved my mother

This is a train whistle at night

This is an Agnes Martin painting

This is a convincing forgery *(2 mimics 1's gesture of an Agnes Martin painting.)*

2: This is a trace amount of plutonium

This is a moment of indecision

This is a field gone fallow

This is the email you never replied to

This is my receding hairline

This is a desecrated holy site

1 and 2 gesture on all lines.

1: This is us listening to the neighbours making love

2: This is them listening to us

1: This is a doubt that plagues me

2: This is a strip bar in Montreal

1: This is a sticky note reminding me to breathe

2: This is the troposphere

1: This is my first day on the job

2: This is my friend Thomas, whom I betrayed

1: This is my friend Mike, whom I loved unrequitedly

2: This is a meal of leftovers

1: This is a reality TV show about wedding dresses

2: This is March

1: This is the birthday party I didn't invite you to

2: This is West Queen West

1: This is our youth

2: This is a pervert

1: This is a baseball field at night

2: This is an algebra problem

1: This is a cashmere turtleneck

1 and 2 continue to gesture on all lines.

1: This is astronomy

    This is a lone deer in a field

    This is its white tail

    This is a long shot

    This is my friend Mark, who lost his mind

    This is you withholding love

    This is a YouTube video of a panda sneezing

    This is a portal

    This is the turning point

    This is gluten-free

    This is a fetish

    This is an after-hours tiki bar

1 and 2 gesture on each other's lines.

2: This is you putting your hand on the small of my back

1: This is a small town with a big church

2: This is a limp dick

1: This is a race car

2: This is a palindrome

1: This is white male privilege

2: This is a syringe

1: This is a rigged ballot

2: This is a wet plastic bag

1 and 2 gesture on their own lines.

1: This is a vicious cycle

2: This is the Command button on your keyboard

1: This is the white chalk in the blackboard eraser

3 and 4 enter and join the performance without interrupting the flow of movement and text.

Hereafter, performers may 'steal' other performer's declarations — speaking a declaration at the same time as the other performer while offering-up their own spontaneous gesture. The effect creates an over-lapping of text but an asynchronicity of gesture. The emergence of these 'steals' should happen gradually but with increasing frequency.

3: This is your kindness

4: This is a man vomiting out of a cab

1: This is the hum of a refrigerator

2: This is lightning seen from space

3: This is a convent of nuns

4: This is a backyard trampoline covered in leaves

1: This is a taco

2: This is a diving bell

3: This is a slow fade to black

4: This is something I whipped together

1: This is April

2: This is a stand of birch trees

3: This is a fragment of Attic pottery

4: This is colonization

1: This is a problematic passage in a history textbook

2: This is a satyr

3: This is the vanishing point

4: This is a charismatic cult leader

1: This is a rat

2: This is the year 1992.

3: This is a cold draft

4: This is a premonition

1: This is the fuzz of a peach

2: This is a portrait of a woman

3: This is my elbow

1: This is Sylvia Plath's oven

4: This is an extinct species

2: This is the Berlin Wall

3: This is a customer service representative

4: This is my best side

1: This is a minor inconvenience

2: This is a derailed train

3: This is a landfill

4: This is naked ambition

1: This is a public service announcement

2: This is summer

3: This is Niagara Falls

4: This is a pinch of salt

1: This is biking drunk

2: This is a sprig of mint

3: This is my mother's cough

4: This is my childhood bedroom

1: This is my mother's cough

2: This is her comb

3: This is the hair in it

1: This is the letter J

2: This is the summer rain

3: This is yesterday

4: This is my mother's cough

1: This is a missing button

2: This is the red glow of an exit sign

3: This is a doodle in the margins

4: This is the stubble on your chin

1: This is where we get off the subway

2: This is a tear in the fabric of reality

3: This is a teardrop

4: This is a destination wedding

1: This is a morgue

2: This is the sound of you in the next room

3: This is the next room

4: This is the view

1: This is the backyard

2: This is our neighbour

3: This is the nearby river

4: This is the town on the other side

1: This is the quiet of the house

2: This is for your own good

3: This is gym class

4: This is the migration of the monarch butterfly

1: This is a plastic surgery clinic in Guadalajara

2: This is an skyscraper designed by Mies van der Rohe

3: This is my father

4: This is a blank piece of paper

1: This is snow blowing upwards

2: This is my father

3: This is an eraser

4: This is my father

1: This is the smell of the earth after rain

2: This is a Styrofoam cup

3: This is me in your womb

4: This is August

1: This is the afterlife

2: This is a snake

3: This is a snake swallowing a mouse

4: This is a Polaroid

1: This is us lying in bed

2: This is a bank robbery

3: This is our unborn daughter

4: This is a bruised banana

1: This is the Prairie sky

2: This is what I will look like when I'm dead

3: This is a dirt road

4: This is a meth lab

1: This is a stunt

2: This is a tectonic plate

3: This is the world slowly tearing apart

4: This is you standing on the earth

1: This is John Glenn orbiting in a spaceship

2: This is the moon

3: This is a lunar eclipse

4: This is a quasar

1: This is an acne scar

2: This is a vegan potluck

3: This is absolutely nothing

4: This is a man taking out the trash

1: This is the Promised Land

2: This is a cab ride through Brooklyn

3: This is static on the radio

4: This is a snuff film

1: This is a pair of scissors

3: This is my Aunt Roberta

4: This is pink nail polish

1: This is a child psychologist

2: This is my mother holding me as a baby

3: This is the Dollarama

4: This is a satellite crossing the night sky

1: This is an upturned kayak

2: This is the Birth of Venus

3: This is my twelfth birthday

4: This is my mother's left breast

1: This is Saturday

2: This is Greece

3: This is a villain from a popular children's television series

4: This is a dirty mattress

1: This is a pirouette

2: This is the married man I slept with in Greece

3: This is a sparkler

4: This is Daniel in the lion's den

1: This is a romantic comedy

2: This is an email you regret sending

3: This is a meme

4: This is a rumour

1: This is an empty office building at night

4: This is your subconscious

1: This is a pus-filled pimple

2: This is an old high school crush

3: This is a can of Orange Crush

4: This is you crushing the can under your foot

1: This is your shoe

2: This is what it smells like

3: This is your toe in my mouth

4: This is you alone with your thoughts

1: This is my mother saying 'good night'

2: This is the colour fuchsia

3: This is the colour fuchsia

4: This is the colour fuchsia

1: This is a surgical scalpel

2: This is my mother saying 'good night'

3: This is a bouquet of tiger lilies

4: This is my nose coated with pollen

1: This is me washing my hands

2: This is a tire swing

3: This is mathematics

4: This is the nightmare where my teeth fall out of my head

1: This is me masturbating at the airport

2: This is Easter Island

3: This is Captain Cook

4: This is a pair of your boxers

1: This is us smoking outside the laundromat

2: This is our laundry combined for the first time in a spin cycle

3: This is the Renaissance

4: This is Jesus Christ

1: This is me putting my number in your phone

2: This is my babysitter, Lisa

3: This is me finding my stolen bike

4: This is a metaphor

1: This is an archive

2: This is an archive

3: This is an airplane passing three miles overhead

4: This is a stewardess

1: This is the in-flight movie

2: This is my mother's fear of flying

3: This is you black-out drunk

4: This is you putting your fist through the wall

1: This is me doing sit-ups in my underwear

2: This is a New Year's resolution

3: This is a disposable camera I never got developed

4: This is a shopping plaza

1: This is the fountain that is never on

2: This is the scum of the earth

3: This is the molten core of the earth

4: This is another planet just like Earth

1: This is the room going dark

Blackout. In the darkness, 5 enters.

2: This is a sound cue

A song begins to play.

The lights gradually return.

3: This is the twenty-six grams a soul weighs

4: This is the twenty-six grams a soul weighs

5: This is the 206 bones of the human body

1: This is the darkness of the tunnel

2: This is the weight of the ocean above you

3: This is cabin pressure

5: This is Earth without my mother

1: This is the shattered screen of an iPhone

2: This is me looking through your bookshelf

3: This is your bad eyesight

4: This is the blue hour

5: This is flesh

1: This is light shifting across the floor

2: This is the hidden compartment in the body where the soul
    is kept

3: This is the hidden compartment in the body where the soul is kept

4: This is the hidden compartment in the body where the soul is kept

1: This is the thing you dread

2: This is the edge of reason

3: This is the thing you dread

4: This is my hand moving across your body on its own accord

5: This is the calm before the storm

1: This is a hole

2: This is the hole we will stick you in

3: This is a burnt field

4: This is a cinder

5: This is my sister

1: This is someone's sister

2: This is a burning witch

3: This is a lodestone

4: This is the riverbed

5: This is a backhoe

1: This is a broken back

2: This is a vertebra

3: This is the truth stretched

4: This is time stopped

3: This is what can be forgiven

5: This is what cannot be forgiven

1: This is what I have forgotten

2: This is us walking on the frozen lake

3: This is what is behind the curtain

4: This is exile

5: This is purgatory

1: This is a swimming lesson

2: This is a pear

3: This is woodsmoke

4: This is a footnote

5: This is a fishing hook

1: This is a gold tooth

2: This is a parallelogram

3: This is me forgetting your name at a party

3 continues to steal lines and gestures from this point onward.

4: This is my social anxiety

5: This is a dropped glass

1: This is an over-eager laugh

2: This is my listening face

4: This is a woman screaming in a movie

5: This is just like the tourist brochure said it would be

1: This is a pinprick

2: This is momentum

4: This is a dropped call

5: This is mist over a field

1: This is early morning soccer practice

2: This is CBC Radio

4: This is my shirt on inside out

5: This is that kitchen scene with the raptors in *Jurassic Park*

1: This is Greta Garbo

2: This is our car being broken into

4: This is a piñata

5: This is a night train

1: This is the sleeper car

2: This is the space between us

4: This is Pangaea

5: This is my enemy

1: This is a worried look

2: This is an inappropriate outburst

4: This is yoga

5: This is modernism

1: This is postmodernism

2: This is a flashlight beam in the dark

5: This is an ex-lover of mine

4: This is a sugar rush

1: This is an ex-lover of mine

2: This is me blocking him on Facebook

4: This is brutalism

5: This is pathos

1: This is a house party

2: This is a garbage bag full of red cups

4: This is you swimming laps under the pool cover

5: This is a bone caught in my throat

1: This is us setting off firecrackers in the driveway

2: This is the ice shelf collapsing

4: This is an iceberg calving

5: This is what history teaches

1: This is an Australopithecus

2: This is what came before

4: This is a rectum

5: This is the shitting out at the end

1: This is the rump

2: This is the dribbling out

4: This is a star colliding with another star

4 continues to steal lines and gestures from this point onward.

5: This is persistence

1: This is Judy

2: This is Judy collapsing on her couch

5: This is Mesopotamia

1: This is a rebuke from the gods

5: This is a convertible

1: This is the wind blowing my hair

2: This is a coastal highway

5: This is a new pair of sunglasses

1: This is your hand on my thigh

2: This is us setting up a tent in the wind

5: This is the neighbour's son

1: This is him running away from home

2: This is his mother coming to our door

5: This is a cop car

1: This is us holding hands, walking through a field

2: This is his shirt by the creek

5: This is the colour beige

1: This is the dirt under my fingernails

2: This is an earthworm

5: This is cigarette ash

1: This is a treehouse

2:   This is a car alarm in the distance at night

5:   This is a dog barking

1:   This is me making myself vulnerable to you

2:   This is a Portuguese custard tart

1:   This is how you pronounce 'Goethe'

5:   This is the CAT scan

2:   This is the dark spot

2 continues to steal lines and gestures from this point onward.

5:   This is the hospital cafeteria

1:   This is a Styrofoam cup of coffee

5:   This is your name over the PA system

1:   This is a discarded pair of plastic gloves

The performers stop gesturing for the proceeding lines.

5:   This is pipe tobacco

1:   This is lemon meringue pie

5:   This is a housefly

1:   This is a glass of gin with two ice cubes

5:   This is a hair in my soup

1:   This is blue Jell-O

5:   This is my hair pulled back in a bun

1:   This is flour on my arms

5: This is licking icing sugar off my fingers

1: This is me sticking my fingers in your vagina

5: This is the taste of you on my lips

1: This is the late afternoon

5: This is me wiping the sweat from my brow

1: This is a hummingbird

5: This is the colour brown

1: This is jazz

5: This is a match

1: This is a coal mine

5: This is a mine collapse

1: This is a horse trapped in the mine

5: This is a glass of milk

1: This is my great-grandfather hanging from the rafters

5: This is syphilis

1: This is ash falling from the sky

5: This is my face in the mirror

1: This is a car in reverse

5 resumes gestures.

5: This is how to fall down a flight of stairs

This is a stubbed toe

This is a black toenail

This is me hitting my thumb with a hammer

This is the nail on my thumb falling off

This is me cutting my hand with a bread knife

This is me wrapping my hand in a dish towel

This is my bruise

This is you pressing it

This is me burning my hand on an element

This is me plunging my hand under cold water

This is me banging my head on the cupboard door

This is me putting ice cubes into a Ziploc bag

This is me slipping on ice

This is me fracturing my tailbone

This is me biting my tongue

This is me chipping a tooth

This is me closing the car door on my dress

This is a cobweb between blades of grass

The proceeding lines are spoken in overlap, with accompanying gestures.

This is how to fill the hours of a day

This is a clementine

This is a song that reminds me of you

This is a song we've forgotten the words to

This is oral tradition

This is oral sex

This is a standing ovation

This is a group of people looking into the sky

This is atonal music

This is an awkward silence

This is coming in for the kiss when you didn't expect it

This is coming in for the kiss when you didn't expect it

This is the flour in the cupboard

This is the mustard in the fridge

This is the centipede in the basement

This is a feather

This is a decade

This is picking back up where we left off

This is my breath in the cold

This is a test

This is a cloud that looks like a face

This is me peeling off a Band-Aid on the streetcar

This is a sprinkler in the suburbs

This is Ezra Pound

This is a duel

This is the last man standing

This is the desert sun setting

This is a horse's skull

This is a Western

This is the Olympics

This is the 100-metre dash

This is us watching in our living room

This is burgundy

This is the sleep in your eyes

This is sleep paralysis

This is traffic

This is a pillow fight

This is my drool on the pillow

This is your morning breath

This is you unfolding the newspaper

This is the smell of newsprint

This is how to disappear

This is water evaporating

This is a suspension bridge

This is the threshold between life and death

1: This is a brick thrown through a window

This is an obtuse angle

This is Antarctica

This is where we met

This is a locked door

This is the colour orange

This is a prophecy

This is an eighties power suit

This is the smell of Windex

This is me, keeping your secret

This is a phone call at four o'clock in the morning

This is a process of elimination

This is a nurse

This is the shade under a car

This is us stuck in the elevator of a Best Western

This is me waiting for you

This is your last chance

This is the absence of God

This is the city

This is September

This is the occult

This is my mother as a little girl

This is the barbarian invasion

This is a box of your things

This is October

This is a meteorite striking Siberia

This is the number four

1, 2, & 4: This is the past

1: This is November

This is the heat of your breath

This is the absence of colour

This is what's possible in the time we have left

This is me whispering your name

This is your name written on the back of a photograph

This is the moment my watch stopped

This is my cheek against your cheek

This is the smell of pine needles

This is the first star of the night

This is the sun on the water

This is you waiting for me

This is where you have been hiding

This is me finding you

1 & 4: This is me

1: This is you

This is us

1 & 3: This is also us

The five performers stand still for a moment. Then, one of them begins to perform an earlier gesture in silence. Then another. Gradually, all five performers are performing their earlier gestures in silence.

This lasts two or three minutes.

Eventually, 2 breaks the silence. During this next section, the gestural score is gradually dropped around 2's line 'This is hard wood.' The performers stand still, except where gestures are noted. Spoken overlaps are designated by the text that appears in the right-hand column. The text in this section should feel reminiscent of fragmented conversation.

2: And this

1: This is

3 & 4: This is light

5: This is

2: Like

4: And likewise

3 & 4: This is

2: Light shining

2: This light

3: The floor

1: Your room

    The floor   2: The wood floor

3: Is this – ?

2: This is hard wood

1: This is the hardest part   2: Would you – ?

2: Thinking

3 & 4: You were

1: Queen of all things

2: Thinking of

1: Queen of liking all things

3: Of and

1: Of all things

4: Considered

3 & 1: Take into

1: Consideration this thing

3: That is

1: Was and is

4: Is and

2: Becoming

3 & 4: Coming and

3: Come upon

4: And apart

1: Put upon

4: And pulled apart

3: Pulled and

2: Pushed out of you

1: Taught me to speak, taught me

4: To walk   5: To run

3: How to count

2: Five on a hand

1: My whole life

2: Everything counts

3: Five on a hand

4: When I was a boy

5: I was fourteen

1: And liking all things

4: Tuesday and

3: Sinking

1 & 4: When I was a boy

5: Shame was placement

3: A place for space meant

5: Basement and base things

4: Teen things and

1: Inner leanings

4: When I was a boy I was Tuesday

3: The colour red

5: And bled profusely

2: Red and refused me

1: Over and over

2: And bruised, see

4: Not calm but loosely

1: In white sheets

4: With loose teeth

2: Stretch the echo

3: Stretch the pattern

4: Stretch the cash

5: Thread the count

1: Count it out

5: Count the corner

1: Count the rest

3: To the bed

2: From the corner

4: And the wall

4 & 5: To wall carpet

1: She got the white house

3: And the better love

2: You could bet yourself

1: One thing

2: You could bet yourself

1: Tuesday

3: You could get yourself

1: Through torn light

2: And blown hot

1: And blown bright

2: The filaments for low rise

1: Low down

2: And likewise

1: And listless

2: And unmade

3: I was a teen of the decade

4: Decked out and dead head

3: Like

2: Likewise

4: A head case

1: Millennial

2: And choices

4: There were choices

1: For this thing

4: Or the choice thing

3: For the bad job

2: And bad fucks

4: The pattern

1: Is movement

2: The pattern

1: Of birds of boys

3: Moping sidelong

1: Long gazes and

3: The long view

5: The listless   3: And that sense of

2: Fortitude

4: How we were before

3: Tuesday

4: How we were

1: My mother

2: She lived

1: If I could just say –

5: She lived

2: My mother

1: One thing   5: My mother was like a
                                        mountain

2: The twenty-first century

3: My mother

1: She lived

4: A woman   3: She'd count it out

2: A twenty-first century   Two

                                        Three

                                        Four

4: And the twentieth   Five

Six

1: She lived

Seven

Eight

2: A woman

1: The twentieth century

5: If things had been different

4: Woman

1: She lived

5: She

2: My mother

4: She lived

5: She could've made something of herself

3: A mother

1: Two sons

2: To mother

1: Alone for most

3: For most

3: A mother

5: But also

1: A fighter

2: In the sense

1: That she fought

3: Light-hearted

4: And painted

1: My mother who lived

2: She was, I said

1 & 3: I love you, I said

4: I love you and love you and love

3: I said

2: Before the night

5: It came

1, 2, & 5: The night

4: The dark

1 & 2: I said

3: The dark

4: I said

5: The twenty-first century

1: Our house   3: It is it had this, like,
                                      white stucco

4: The street

5: The shade

4: And under the cars

1: The shade   2: It was never like that

5: The cat

1: The trees beyond

5: The children

1: The yards

2: The dinners she made

3: The friends she kept   5: Until I got the call

4: The fell

1: The tree, the spot

2: The breast

3: The bones

1: The dark

2, 3, & 5: The dark

4: The dark inside

1: That felled

4: Her veins

1: Like trees   3: The shade

2: And felled the night

1: To sleep

4: She said

2: The thing that is

1: And was the thing, it is the shape

3: This shape

4: This thing

5: Right here

1: The colour green

2: It is like this

They all clap.

2: It is like this

1, 4, and 5 begin to sing a soft, simple melody of their own devising.

3: This is me alone in the world *(gestures)*

2: This is me alone in the world *(gestures)*

3: This is a boy *(gestures)*

2: Singing

3: In the yard

2: In his head

3: And aloud

2: In my head I was allowed to sing imaginary songs

3: They would go kind of like –

2: That did not yet exist

3: To consider

2: Not to exist

3: But sing songs of existence

In my head in the yard

2: In the world

3: In the world

3: In the suburbs

2: Of the world

3: In the shade

2: Below the car

3: Below the sky

2: Below the blue

3: It is a comfort

2: Of course

3: It is comfort

2: The blue

3: Thing that speaks

2: And does not speak

3: Her eyes that are blue

2: And yet not blue and yet

3: Not spoken

2: And not heard

3: The flock that is

2: Not home

3: And unmade

2: The sound of the dog in the yard

3: It is like this

1 and 5 drop out, leaving 4 to continue to the melody alone.

3: He goes like this

   The dog that is me

1: He's in the yard

3: At night he walks

    And goes like this

1: And this alone

3: And this at night

1: And in the yard

3: He asks himself

1: Where is the grass   5: Where is my home

1: And where are the birds

2: Where is my home

3: They do not flock

5: Where is my mother

1: They do not cry   5: If not in blue

3: Where is my mother   2: If not at home

1: If not a dog

3: If not the sound of

1: The furnace roar   5: Where is my mother

3: The sound of fury

1: The sound of shade   2: Consider if you will

3: And under the car

4: Sound the alarm

1: Sound the distance   2: Come down now

4: Sound the alarm

3: The sound

1: Of distance

3: The sound of

4: Wind

1: On wind

3: On white

1: On lawns

3: Freshly cut

1: On fields

3: On malice

2: On fog on fields

1: On morning jogs

3: It snags

1: And jogs

3: To jog

1: In the mouth

2: Of a stranger

1: All things

4: All signs

1: I keep an eye

3: Blue colour

2: All things

2: Comin' down comin' now
   down comin' down

5 & 2: Your name

1: A call

5: A sign

65

1: I keep my eyes peeled

5: Blue colour

1: I keep hoping

3: Blue colour

1: I keep blue watch

3 & 5: Blue colour

1: I keep an eye on your soul

5: But not bother

1: I keep an eye on the time

2: But no bother

1: And if this is what is

3: Then don't bother

1: And if I am asleep

3: Then I'm tired

1: And if I am awake

3: Then I'd rather

1: Be with you

3: Than alone

1: In this yard

5: Clean the gutters

2: You called them

5: The eavestroughs

2: You called in   1: Hello?

5: Some favours

3: And for a while

2: There was quiet

3: For a while

5: The highway was closed

1: Just the wind

3: Collecting its toll

5: Its tax

1: On the soul

4's melody drops out.

2: The heart

1: Shucks and jives and

3: Doubles in time

2: My heart

3: Doubles in time

5: Three and four   2: Look

3: And double in time

2: Here it is

5: Thanks for the laughs

1: And the scraps of your time

3: Look

(Beat)

1: Look at me

3: Look   2: I'm old

4: Just   3: Look at me

5: I feel fucking old, man

4: Sometimes

5: You know   2: I just

(Pause)

1: That's the only way I can describe it

2: Tired

3: Of the world

4: Of   2: Being in the world

5: My body

3: What I can do

4: With this body

1: All bodies through which

2: I've come

3: Known to myself   1: And

4: All bodies, all faces

5: All shades   2: Coming

1: His

3: Wet

4: Slick

2: Slip

1: His tongue

2: The heat of his

5: Breath on my neck   3: So – hot

1: Kiss and licked

4: Twice, three times   1: My age

2: He had a wife   3: All the lovers

1: I've known

2: And younger

4: The bodies through which

5: I've known my own

3: Carpenters, lawyers

1: A few actors obviously   4: Yup

3: Gross

5: Sunday drives

2: The moisture of our

5: Bodies in heat

1: Rock rock   3: Rocking

2: Rock hard

5: Fuck

4: That was –

1: Sunday

3: That was

2: Good

1: That was a good life

2: That's some good news

5: That's the gospel   3: That's the gospel truth

1: That's the thing

4: That's the couch   2: – if you wanna take a seat

1: Just –

3: Collapse on the couch

1: If the couch is there

2: If the couch is not

1: Collapse elsewhere

2: If your heart is collapsible

1: I give you permission

2: Comin' down now

4: To disappear

3: To the low lands

1: Where the ancestors

4: If we can call them ancestors

1: Once told us

2: Look

3: Watch and

1: If you want to know

2 &3: The earth   4: What we were

5: Just

1: Shut up

ALL: And listen

They all listen.

The performers take their time with the text for the next page or two.

1: Been

2: Been there

1: I was there

3: I've been there

1: I hear you

3: I've been there

1: And I hear you

5: Listen

They all listen.

4: The shape of this movement

3: Is motion

4: The weight of the world

3: Is water

4: And revealed in the water

3: Is movement

1: And the quiet you call dawn

4: And the roar you call water   2: Water comin' down
                                          comin' down now

3: The boy you called young

5: I was ten then and the water

4: You called Niagara Falls

3: And you were four times my age

2: And the roar

5: How she held me

2: The mist of years

3: The things that we were

5: Holding my weight

3: And the wind stripped us bare

2: My young ten mind

3: And chastened my years

2: And Marilyn Monroe

3: And the long drive home

2: Soft rock and the back seat

3: And the secrets you'd keep

2: And not keep

3: And not but by the mercy of God

4: The summer

3: The winter

4: The world

3: We made a pact

4: That if I fell

3: You would catch me

4: That if I fell

5: And vice versa

3: Your bedside

2: The sheets

3: The corner

2: The white

5: Your face

4: And vice versa

2: The summer

3: The fall

4: And vice versa

5: This is the corrective

1: Come

4: Come home

1 & 2: She said

4: Come home and stay   3: Fucking hell

2: For a while

1: She said

4: Come home and I said

1: I'm in the city

2: For a while

4: But no there was no

3: Time

5: It turned out

1: She said   3: How am I supposed to accommodate that?

4: Come

1: Before it turned

5: And stay a while

1: And I said thanks

4: But no

2: But

1: But how could I know

5: At the time

1: At the time on

4: Wednesday there were five things to do

1: Call the bank

3: Call it off

4: Call home

1: Wherever that was

2: Wherever you were

5: In the world

3: The smell of gasoline

5: Was turquoise

1: And then

2: Collapse

3: You

2: Collapsed

1: And I –   4: I distinctly recall

3: The phone call

2: Come home

1: In the dark

4: Dark dark   3: On the couch

1: Dark and   2: Dry

4: In the dark

2: Dry cough

1: On the couch   5: How I found her

4: Orange peels

1: And tissue

3: Orange peels   5: A glass

1: And a glass of water

3: Water is

2: The giver

1: Wash your body

  Clean and raw

  Skin in the tub

  Hair in the drain

  Everything drained

  All of you drained

5: In the tub

1: Body clean and slip

5: Slip and hit

1: Your head catch   4: Shit

5: Your body as it slips

1: A squeak and let slip a squeal

4: And split

3: The head

1: Small split the crack

5: The tiles your head

1: The blood in the tub

5: The drain

2: The hot   3: All things now

1: Water falling

4: The world   3: All things in play

1: The sound of

2: The world collapsing   4: This sound

3: That no one hears

1: Something like this

2 & 3: Something like

3 makes a noise.

1: Something like

They all make the noise.

1: Something like dying

5: But not death

1: Itself

5: No

1: Not itself

4: Never myself

2: Love you still but

4: Look   5: I haven't been myself since

1: They took you

2: Your body just

3: Just

2: Ash   5: Your body

4: Falling

1: Your body in the

   Keyhole slot

2: Of the wall

1: Granite wall

   Granite

   Body without

3: A body

1: In the wall

   What the body recalls

1: In death

2: A breath   4: Hot on your neck

1: To be sure   3: Her neck

2: You lived

1: To be sure

2: If I can say

1: One thing

4: For sure

1: It's that

2: You lived

5: You are you were

1: She was she loved

2: And loved a dog

3: And loved two boys

5: A house a man

4: Once or twice

1: Enough to know   5: I love you

2: To say I do

1: I love you and

3: Always ever

1: Under white light 2: The hospital gown

4: White skies

5: And passages of books

2: And halls in

3: Hospitals and

2: Bathroom stalls

3: And held hands

2: Shaking   4: Her hands

1: Were shaking

2: Shake shake

1: And wait

5: And dream of you

1: And wondering

3: How is this to be

2: Let me show you

They hold up their hands.

2: Vision of mercy

1: Vision of light

3: Vision of her back

4: On the beach

3: The smell of her blood

4: Her hair in the drain   5: My throat

1: The hair on our heads

3: The sound in my throat

4: A wish

2: A ghost pale

3: A dawn wind drawn thin

4: The burr on my jeans

1: And nothing beneath

2: Clung thick and wind

1: Lithe and lose and even death

2: Is an option   3: I want you to know that
everything you can think of

4: In the city everything

2: Is an option

1: Everything   3: Everything is an option

5: Is in play

4: Even play itself

1: Even you and me   2: Eight, nine

5: In just ten easy payments

2: Forgiveness in ten and eleven

1: And even now

2: I open myself to the city

1: To the distinct possibility

2: Of the first quarter

3: Of the twenty-first century

1: And even at this late hour

2: The shape of this movement

3: Is motion

4: The weight of the world

3: Is water

5: And revealed in the water

1: Is movement

*4 begins to sing his song from earlier. 3 begins a slow vogue dance.
She is eventually joined by 2.*

It is a sensual and sublime moment.

The song ends.

3: Heaven

    Heaven

    Heaven

    Heaven heaven

    Heaven heaven heaven

    Heaven heaven heaven heaven heaven heaven heaven
heaven heaven heaven heaven heaven heaven heaven heaven
heaven heaven heaven heaven heaven heaven heaven heaven
heaven heaven heaven heaven heaven heaven heaven hev en
heavenheavenheaven even even heaven heaven hev en heaven
hev heaven heaven heaven even hev heaven haven *(laughs, turns
to the others)* if you say it enough times heaven heaven heaven
even heaven heaven heavenheaven evenevenheeven it stops –
heaven heaveneveneven *(laughs)* heaven heaven heavenheavenheaven heaven –

1: Heaven is

3: If I may say

1: Bullshit

2: Heaven is   4: Like

1: Let me tell you

2: It's a game changer

1: Hear me out   4: Light through your eyelids

5: The last thing

3: On your mind I know

2: It's not real

3: Okay   5: I don't need this information

2: Let me tell you first hand

1: Hear me out

5: Look

1: Here is my hand

They raise their right hands.

3: Here is my hand

1: I believe in it

3: I have confirmed it

1: With the authorities

1: Hear me out

3: Here   1: Here we are without

4: We

5: Are

3: Without

1: The people who were

2: Until a very short time ago

3: Perhaps just before the winter

5: The first snowfall

4: The snow

1: Blowing upwards

3: If they saw the snow   2: If they

5: Blowing upwards

2: They may have known

3: Tiny miracles

1: It was near

2: They may have felt

1: The nights

5: Growing longer

4: They may have felt

1: Your love

3: They may have seen the snow

5: Blowing upwards

1: But you cannot be sure

2: After the fact

3: Mostly   2: Running   5: Falling

4: Personally   1: Jumping to conclusions

5: I have doubts

1: I know   2: I was running

3: Always have

1: Even as a child

5: Running   3: The water

4: To do everything

1: Just to grab a cup   2: So afraid

4: In case it suddenly wasn't there

1: Water from the tap   3: Running

4: If it suddenly wasn't there

5: My bed

2: Your love

3: Just fine

1: Thanks

4: Okay then

1: Well

ALL: Bye

2: Bye for now

1: Bye

3: See you

4: Goodbye   2: And thanks

5: Okay then   2: For everything, I mean it's been

1: Well

ALL EXCEPT 2: Goodbye

1: Love you

3: See you later

5: See you

4:	Hopefully

1:	Thanks for everything

3:	Bye now

2:	Bye

4:	Give a good shake

5:	Give a good

1:	Shake

2:	And if I could just say

ALL:	Shake

3:	Two things

4:	Shake

3:	Two things

5:	Shake shake

1:	Three things

ALL:	Shake

1:	Three things

4:	Shake shake shake

5:	Three things

ALL:	Shake

5:	Three things

2:	Shake shake shake

1:	Four things

ALL: Shake shake momma shake shake

2: Four things

1: Shake shake momma shake shake

3 & 4: Five, on a hand

(All clap)

ALL: Shake shake momma shake momma shake shake

2 & 5: Five, on a hand

(All clap)

ALL: Shake shake momma shake momma shake shake

5: This is the corrective

Everyone incants the following lines together, stomping on the underlined 'shakes' and clapping immediately after the line 'Five on a hand.'

This repeats fifteen times, with gradual choreographic variations. A joyous ritual emerges, which grows increasingly ecstatic. Eventually a frenzied freeform dance breaks out. But no matter how far the ritual escalates, the performers never lose the rhythm they establish with the stomps and claps.

ALL: *Shake*

    Two things

    Shake shake

    Two things

Shake

Three things

Shake shake shake

Three things

Shake

Three things

Shake

Three things

Shake shake momma shake shake

Four things

Shake shake momma shake shake

Five, on a hand *(all clap)*

Shake shake momma shake momma shake shake

Five, on a hand *(all clap)*

(x15)

5: This is the corrective

ALL: *Shake* with tears

   Shake with tears momma

2: This is the record

ALL: *Shake* with tears

   And

   And

And *shake*

With laughs

Shake shake with good laughs momma

Shake

Three things

Shake shake shake

Three things

Shake with tears shake shake with tears

Shake with tears

Shake (final stomp)

The ritual is now over. The performers are exhausted.

3: This is what grief looks like

ALL: Shake shake shake

3: One quarter into the millennium

5: This is what

1: This is what death looks like

ALL: Shake

3: One quarter into the millennium

5: This is what

1: I look like

2: This is what

1: This is what I look like

3: One quarter into the millennium

They all hum, as 1 performs a monologue.

1: The bus was late

   I was waiting for it but it was late

   I reached into my pocket to grab my phone

   to check the time

   but my pocket was empty

   In my mind's eye I could suddenly see my phone

   sitting on my bedside table still charging

   I had not fuck I had not taken it with me fuck

   I had my hand in my pocket

   when I looked up and I saw her jogging toward me

   Jogging out of the house in her nightgown and slippers

   She was home because she was in the midst of chemo

   No longer working

   Bald and jogging toward me

   This is my mother I thought to myself

   This is her love

   Jogging with my phone toward me

   Bald and in her slippers

   This is her love

   This is a declaration of her love

She arrived at the bus stop and handed me my phone

She handed me my phone

She said: *This is your phone*

As if I didn't recognize it

She handed me my phone

and kissed me on the cheek

Kissed me on the cheek just the one time

ALL: One time

1: Once on the cheek

And then I watched her walk back toward our house

The two minutes of her walk

Back toward our house

And then watched her walk

back into our house

Where she lived the rest of the day

Where she lived one more day

Until I returned home

Lights slowly fade as they hum.

Darkness.

End of piece.

Declarations in rehearsal

Acknowledgements

Firstly, my heartfelt thanks to the ensemble of the original production: Liz Peterson, Jennifer Dahl, Danielle Baskerville, Philip Nozuka, and Robert Abubo, for their tireless, generous spirits. I am also indebted to our production team: Kimberly Purtell, Ashley Ireland, A. J. Laflamme, Greg Dougherty, Heather Landon, Lee Milliken, Lynanne Sparrow, Sally Roberts, and Ming Wong. To all of the staff at Canadian Stage, from publicity and marketing to box office to the front of house team, thank you for bringing *Declarations* to life. An extra special thank you to Matthew Jocelyn and Sherrie Johnson for years of collaboration and support.

There were a number of people and institutions along the way who believed in *Declarations* and helped push it forward. Particular thanks to Colin Rivers, Luke Holbrook, Birgit Schreyer Duarte, Erin Brubacher, Evalyn Parry, and Why Not Theatre. Also to Norman Armour, Joyce Rosario, the PuSh Festival, and the ensemble of performers who gifted me the opportunity to try out an early incarnation of *Declarations* back in 2016.

Before *Declarations* was a performance, it was a video piece, performed by Liz Peterson. This video, and everything that came after, would not have existed without Sam Lebel-Wong. Sam, thank you so much for your faith in my idea, your artistry, and your friendship, I am eternally grateful. A big hug, also, to Michael DiCarlo and everyone else who worked on this video.

Now *Declarations* exists as a beautiful book, thanks to the incomparable team at Coach House Press: Alana Wilcox, Crystal Sikma, Jessica Rattray, and Ricky Lima. Also, my immense gratitude to Andrew B. Myers for his perfect photograph.

Finally, I would like to thank my family: James, Andrew, Dad, Granny, Gramp. And of course, Zoikie.

About the Author

Jordan Tannahill is a play-wright, director, and author. In 2016, he was described by the *Toronto Star* as being 'widely celebrated as one of Canada's most accomplished young play-wrights, filmmakers, and all-round multidisciplinary artists.' His plays have been translated  into multiple languages and honoured with a number of prizes including the Governor General's Literary Award for Drama and several Dora Mavor Moore Awards. Jordan's films and multimedia performances have been presented at festivals and galleries such as the Toronto International Film Festival, the Art Gallery of Ontario, and the Tribeca Film Festival. From 2012 to 2016, Jordan and William Ellis ran the influential underground art space Videofag out of their home in Toronto's Kensington Market. In 2017, his play *Late Company* transferred to London's West End while his virtual reality performance *Draw Me Close*, a co-production between the National Theatre (UK) and the National Film Board of Canada, premiered at the Venice Biennale. Jordan's work in dance includes collaborations with Christopher House and Akram Khan. His debut novel, *Liminal*, was published by House of Anansi Press in January 2018.

Typeset in Amethyst Pro.

Printed at the Coach House on bpNichol Lane in Toronto, Ontario, on Zephyr Antique Laid paper, which was manufactured, acid-free, in Saint-Jérôme, Quebec, from second-growth forests. This book was printed with vegetable-based ink on a 1973 Heidelberg KORD offset litho press. Its pages were folded on a Baumfolder, gathered by hand, bound on a Sulby Auto-Minabinda and trimmed on a Polar single-knife cutter.

Edited by Alana Wilcox
Designed by Crystal Sikma
Cover art by Andrew Myers
Rehearsal photo by Nathan Kelly
Author photo by Alejandro Santiago

Coach House Books
80 bpNichol Lane
Toronto ON M5S 3J4
Canada

416 979 2217
800 367 6360

mail@chbooks.com
www.chbooks.com